DISCOVER THE **MOST AMAZING TANKS** ON EARTH!

MEGA BOOK OF
TANKS

ALLIGATOR
www.alligatorbooks.co.uk

© 2006 Alligator Books Limited

Published by
Alligator Books Limited
Gadd House, Arcadia Avenue
London N3 2JU

Printed in China

CONTENTS

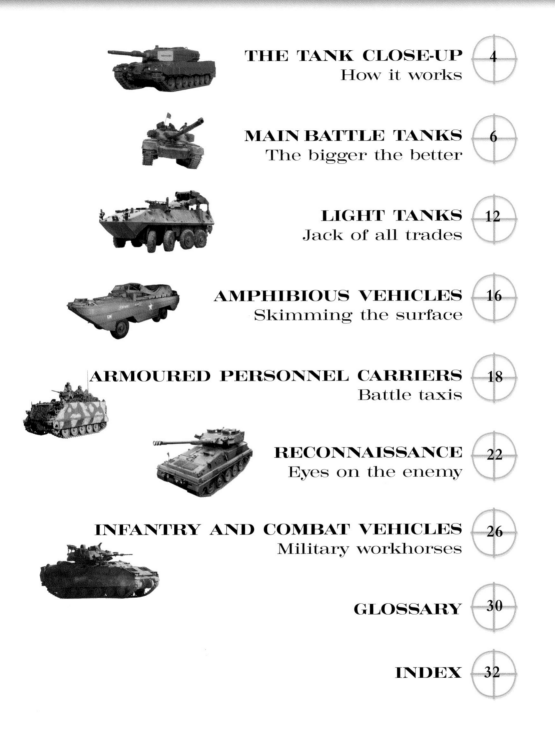

Tanks have played a role in all the major ground battles since 1916. The first British tanks were little armour-plated tractors with basic field-gun or machine-gun armaments. Since World War II (1939–1945), there have been many improvements to tank designs, and their huge size and elaborate designs became surplus to requirements. On the following pages you can find out about all kinds of tracked vehicles, from the earliest armoured personnel carriers (APCs) right through to the very latest combat tanks.

MEGA MBT
No single weapons system on the battlefield has to face such an array of threats as the main battle tank (MBT). These vehicles face attack by aircraft, other tanks and armoured fighting vehicles (AFVs), mines and ground-launched anti-tank guided weapons.

Observation periscope

The main armament of this Leopard 2 MBT is a 120 mm smoothbore gun.

The main gun of the Leopard 2 can fire a range of ammunition, including the new armour-piercing, fin-stabilised, discarding sabot (APFSDS) rounds.

Track

Ernest Swinton

As a British war correspondent on the Western Front during World War I, Sir Ernest Dunlop Swinton had witnessed the deaths of thousands of Allied infantry soldiers at the hands of German machine gunners. Swinton first suggested the development of what became known as the 'tank' when he saw a tractor towing a gun. The British military developed a prototype, and then Prime Minister Lloyd George immediately authorised full-scale production. These early tanks came off the assembly line too late for use in the Somme offensive, but their battlefield debut came at Flers in September 1916. They have been used ever since.

LIGHTEN UP!

At the beginning of World War II, a typical tank such as the British Cruiser Mk IV weighed around 15 tonnes. By the end of the war, tanks such as the German Tiger 11 weighed a massive 71.1 tonnes! During the 1950s and 60s, manufacturers lowered the weight of their vehicles to 40 tonnes to increase their mobility.

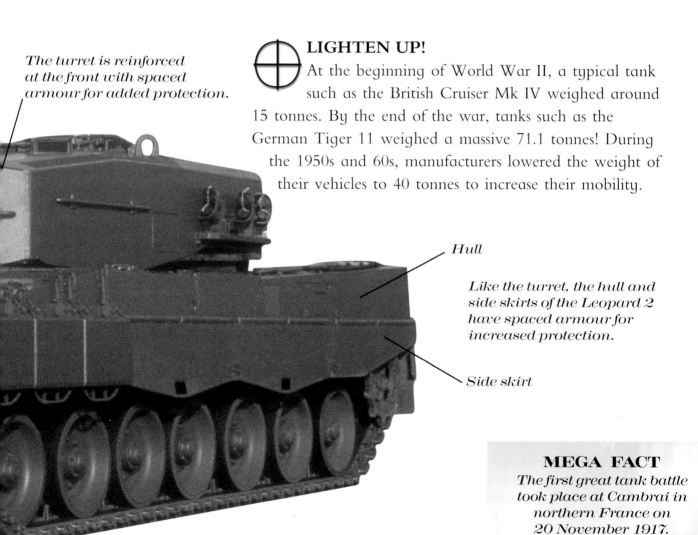

The turret is reinforced at the front with spaced armour for added protection.

Hull

Like the turret, the hull and side skirts of the Leopard 2 have spaced armour for increased protection.

Side skirt

MEGA FACT
The first great tank battle took place at Cambrai in northern France on 20 November 1917.

MAIN BATTLE TANKS

Until 1916, many of the great battles were fought and won by ships at sea. Ground combat was hard work for soldiers with limited weapons and mobility. The tank changed life on the battlefield dramatically. With the tank's combination of firepower, manoeuvrability and protection, soldiers could travel into previously inaccessible areas. One tank could cause more damage than a whole company of foot soldiers. But tank manufacturers had to strike a balance between armour, firepower and mobility to be truly effective fighting machines.

MEGA BATTLE
During the Battle of Kursk, from July to September in 1943, 2,700 German tanks fought against 3,300 Soviet tanks.

WHAT'S IN A NAME?
How did the tank get its name? One theory suggests that when the first tanks were shipped from Britain to France, hidden under canvas sheets, curious soldiers were told that they were transporting large water tanks.

Little Willie

The first prototype tank, or 'land ship' as it was then known, was demonstrated to British military experts on 11 September 1915. The prototype, called 'Little Willie', weighed around 14 tonnes and was powered by a Daimler engine. On even terrain, the 3.6-metre-long track frames carried a three-man crew at an average speed of just over 4.8 km/h. But the average speed dropped to less than 3.2 km/h over uneven terrain, and Little Willie could not cross broad trenches.

ARMOUR AND ATTACK

Major improvements in tank armour appeared in the 1980s. Some armour systems make anti-tank missiles explode outward on impact. New armament includes guns that fire guided missiles and shells made of hard materials that punch straight through enemy tanks.

I CAN DO THAT!

Modern armoured fighting vehicles (AFVs) have largely replaced the big, heavy tanks of the past. Smaller and lighter than their predecessors, many AFVs can perform multiple roles during combat and peacetime ground operations.

MEGA BATTLE

During the Middle East War in 1967, 1,000 Israeli tanks battled against 2,050 Egyptian, Jordanian and Syrian tanks.

CHIEFTAIN MBT

The Chieftain Main Battle Tank (MBT) has been one of the most successful postwar tanks, with its heavy steel armour and large 120 mm main gun. The Chieftain MBT was phased out of the British Army in 1996, after 30 years service. A number of specialised variants are still in service, including the Armoured Recovery Vehicle (ARV), Armoured Vehicle-Launched Bridge (AVLB) and Armoured Vehicle Royal Engineer (AVRE).

M1 ABRAMS MBT

The first Abrams M1 MBT was in operation by 1982. Three years later, there were 2,380 M1s. During Operation Desert Storm, the United States military deployed nearly 2,000 M1s to the Persian Gulf, where they destroyed most of the Iraqis' Soviet tank fleet. The 105 mm main gun on the M1 and the 120 mm gun on the M1A1 and M1A2, combined with the powerful turbine engine and near impenetrable armour, means that the M1 Abrams can attack or defend against large concentrations of heavily armoured forces.

MERKAVA MK3 BAZ

After years of hands-on combat experience in the Arab–Israeli conflict, Major-General Israel Tal designed the Merkava MBT. Most modern MBTs have the engine at the

rear, but the Merkava has the engine at the front of the tank. This provides a special protective umbrella for the crew. The Merkava Mk 1 entered service against Syrian forces in 1982. The Merkava Mk 3 entered service in 1990. New features include a higher-power main gun, a laser-warning system and new armour, suspension, and transmission systems.

LECLERC MBT

The Leclerc MBT came into service with the French Army in 1992 and the United Arab Emirates in 1995. This tank includes a gun with an automatic loading system, which makes it possible to fire when the tank is moving and at a rate of up to six shots per minute. The Leclerc can engage enemy vehicles on any terrain, day or night, whatever the weather. The multipurpose armoured protection, stealth features, agility and long-range capability make the Leclerc a truly awesome fighter.

9

T-90 MBT

The T-90 entered production in 1994 and is the latest in the T-series of Russian tanks. The main armament is the 125 mm 2A46M smoothbore gun, which can fire a range of ammunition, including laser-guided 9M119M 'Refleks' anti-tank missiles and AT-11 Sniper anti-tank guided missiles (ATGM). The T-90 has a four-stroke diesel engine with a multi-fuel capability. Like all Russian MBTs, the T-90 creates its own smoke screen by spraying diesel fuel into the main exhaust outlet.

MEGA FACT
The Soviet Army was the first military power to develop a three-crew tank with an autoloader, replacing the loader to save weight and height.

ARIETE MBT

The Italian Army employs the 54,000 kilogram Ariete tank to engage stationary and moving targets. The main gun is a 44-calibre 120 mm smoothbore gun, which fires armour-piercing, fin-stabilised, discarding sabot (APFSDS) and high explosive, anti-tank (HEAT) rounds. A nuclear, biological and chemical (NBC) protection system guards against NBC attack. The tank is powered by a turbocharged Fiat V-12 MTCA 12-cylinder diesel engine.

Sherman Tank World War II

The United States M4 Sherman medium tank was the major AFV of the Allied forces during World War II, serving on every major front. By the end of the war, factory workers in 11 assembly plants in the USA were turning out almost 2,000 tanks a month. Each M4 weighed about 30,500 kilograms and carried a crew of five soldiers. The main armament was a 75 mm M3 gun, with a 5 cm M3 smoke mortar in the turret roof and several machine guns fixed in various positions on the body of the vehicle.

LEOPARD 2 MBT

The Leopard series of German tanks were developed in the 1960s. The Leopard 1 was first produced in 1963 and its upgrade, Leopard 2, followed in 1979. Leopard 2 includes a new 120 mm L55 smoothbore gun to replace the shorter 120 mm L44 smoothbore gun on the Leopard 1. The new armament supports the new APFSDS-T ammunition. The Leopard 2 also includes the Integrated Command and Information System (ICIS) and can be sealed for NBC warfare. More than 8,000 Leopard 1 and 2 MBTs have been fielded by 18 countries, including 11 NATO nations and Australia, Austria, Brazil and Chile.

MEGA FACT
Late-model Soviet tanks have an interior lining of a synthetic material containing lead, which provides some protection against nuclear fallout, neutron radiation and electromagnetic pulse (EMP).

LIGHT TANKS

Armies around the world have invested a lot of time and money developing tracked vehicles that are smaller, lighter, easier to crew, cheaper to maintain and more affordable than the heavily armed and armoured MBTs. Light tanks are often deployed in situations where MBTs are impracticle or unavailable, for example, against unsophisticated enemy vehicles and in policing operations. Light tanks first came into service in the 1950s and 1960s. Many are still used today, although they are often described as destroyers or reconnaissance vehicles.

MEGA FACT

In 1952, Soviet PT76 amphibious vehicles were the first tanks to use hydrojets as a means of water propulsion.

MEGA FACT

The Soviet Union and communist Eastern European formed the Warsaw Pact in response to the admission of West Germany into NATO.

Alvis Striker SP ATGW

As soon as tanks appeared in World War I, armies began working on ways to stop or destroy these machines using anti-tank weapons. Anti-tank guided weapons (ATGWs) may be single-shot, one-man weapons, or they may have a crew, such as the British Alvis Striker SP ATGW. The Alvis Striker fires a wire-guided, Swingfire anti-tank missile. Most modern ATGWs are wire-guided. This reliable guidance system cannot be jammed by the enemy.

⊕ MULTI-WHEELED MOBILITY

For many years, most wheeled armoured fighting vehicles (AFVs) outside the former Warsaw Pact countries were of the 4x4 type. However, there has been a trend towards developing 6x6 and 8x8 AFVs with increased payloads and greater cross-country mobility.

MEGA FACT
In 1904, the first armoured car — the Charron Girardot et Voigt — was built in France.

⊕ LIGHT AFVs

Many countries already use light AFV fleets. Wheeled vehicles such as the Light Armoured Vehicle LAV-25 (shown left) have lower operating costs than most MBTs, and they have greater strategic mobility and are also easier to transport by air.

LAV-25

The US Army and Marine Corps was assigned the first LAV-25s in 1983. These are all-terrain, all-weather 8x8 vehicles have a maximum speed of 100 km/h on the ground. As an amphibious vehicle, the LAV-25 is powered by two propellers mounted at the rear of the hull, which provide a top speed of 10.4 km/h through the water.

M24 CHAFFEE LIGHT

The M24 Chaffee is considered to be one of the best light tanks of World War II. The first of these vehicles was produced in 1943, and the US Army placed a large order soon after trials proved the effectiveness of these new tanks. By the end of the war, the manufacturers Cadillac and Massey Harris had produced a total of 4,070 M24s. The first to reach Europe in late 1944 were used as reconnaissance vehicles. The M24 Chaffee remained in service in the US Army until 1953, to be replaced by the M41 Bulldog.

AMX-13 LIGHT TANK/RECCE VEHICLE

Work on the French AMX-13 began a year after the end of World War II, and it has proved to be one of the most successful postwar tank designs in the world. Originally designed to be transportable by aircraft, providing airborne forces with medium-fire support, the AMX-13 soon became the standard light tank of the French Army, where it was employed as a tank destroyer and reconnaissance vehicle. All AMX-13 have a similar layout, with the driver sitting front left, the engine to his right and turret at the rear.

MEGA FIRST
The first commercial tracked vehicle was a converted steam agricultural tractor built by the American Holt Manufacturing Company in 1906.

T-26

The T-26 light tank was the Soviet version of the Vickers-Armstrong 6-tonne Tank. Initially, the T-26 was both a single-turret and twin-turret tank, but production centred on the single-turret version after 1933. By the time production ceased in 1939, more than 6,500 T-26 variants had rolled off the assembly lines.

AMPHIBIOUS VEHICLES

Armies need their tanks to have amphibious capabilities so that they can continue advancing without the need for cumbersome and slow-moving bridging equipment to help them cross water courses. Some light vehicles can float, while most MBTs rely on flotation mechanisms to help them cross the water. However, most tanks are capable of submerged fording, which means that they can cross rivers approximately 2.2 metres in depth.

DUKW

The DUKW was a large six-wheel-drive amphibious landing craft first used by the US Army and Marine Corps in World War II. This vehicle proved to be so reliable that the United States manufactured more than 20,000 DUKWs during the conflict. The DUKW was used to ferry equipment from supply ships in transport areas offshore to supply depots and fighting units on the beach. It could maintain a speed of 80 km/h on land and 5 knots at sea.

Cadillac Gage Stingray LT

Textron Marine & Land Systems (formerly Cadillac Gage) developed the Stingray as an extremely mobile light tank with the firepower of a MBT. The Stingray fires a range of ammunition, including British and US APFSDS rounds and NATO 105 mm ordnance. In terms of mobility, the Stingray can climb gradients of up to 60 per cent and cross vertical obstacles up to 82 cm high and water depths to 107 cm. These features make this tank an attractive addition to the armies of countries throughout the world.

BRDM-2

The BRDM-2 is a fully armoured, four-wheel drive, amphibious reconnaissance vehicle with a 140-horsepower, V-8 engine and full NBC protection capability. The basic BRDM-2 reconnaissance vehicle is distinguished by its turret. The conical turret, which mounts two machine guns, has no top-hatch opening. This model carries a crew of four soldiers: the commander, gunner, driver and co-driver. The BRDM-2 was first deployed in 1966, and it has generally replaced the earlier BRDM in the former Soviet Union and other Warsaw Pact nations.

Many modern tracked vehicles used by today's armies serve different purposes and can be classified under more than one type. For example, the German Marder and the British Warrior are classed as both APCs and Armoured Infantry Fighting Vehicles (AIFVs). Wheeled APCs are widely used in United Nations peace-keeping operations, because they protect against rifle and machine-gun fire as well as shell fragments.

MEGA FACT

The idea of an amoured fighting vehicle (AFV) appeared in rough drawings by the Italian artist Leonardo da Vinci in 1482. Leonardo's AFV was propelled by a crew that operated geared hand cranks and fired muskets through slits.

Hidden Armour

All tanks and AFVs are camouflaged to blend in with their surroundings, which makes them more difficult to see from a distance, especially by passing enemy aircraft. Extra armour is also added to many tanks to protect them against enemy fire, but this increased weight inevitably slows them down. The M981 (shown right) is an M113 series tank with extra armour added to the top. To avoid adding too much weight to the vehicle, the armour is made of aluminium.

TANK TRANSPORTERS

The British Ministry of Defence has placed an order with the consortium FASTTRAX to manufacture a new fleet of huge tank transporters. The transporters – known as Heavy Equipment Transporters (HETs) – are based on the US tank-transporter system with a similar name and will be collectively capable of carrying more than 90 tanks into combat zones at speeds of up to 80 km/h. The FASTTRAX consortium will own, operate and maintain the fleet of 92 transporters. The service came into effect in 2003.

> **MEGA FACT**
> *The US Army has purchased 1,179 Heavy Equipment Transporter System (HETS) trucks and trailers since the contract was completed in 1992.*

A DUCK TO WATER

A number of specialised versions of the M113 series are in service with the Norwegian Army, including the NM142. This tank has a one-man Armoured Launching Turret with two Tube-Launched, Optically-Tracked, Wire Guided (TOW) ATGW in the ready-to-launch position. This amphibious vehicle is propelled through the water by the movement of its tracks.

M113

The first M113 tanks were operational by 1962. With more than 80,000 vehicles built in the USA, and M113 production also under licence in Italy, this tank is now the most widely used military vehicle in the world – in service in 50 countries. The M113 was the first AFV to be built using aircraft-quality aluminium. The General Motors Detroit Diesel 6V-53 engine has an output of 275 horsepower at 2,800 revolutions per minute.

MEGA FACT
The British War Office saw the first true AFV in 1902, when the Simms 'War Car' was demonstrated to the military.

WARRIOR APC/AIFV

The armament of the Warrior can be adapted for a range of combat conditions, but a 30 mm Rarden cannon and a 7.62 Boeing M242 chain gun are typical specifications. There are a number of variants of the Warrior, including a mechanised recovery vehicle and mortar carrier. As an AIFV, the Warrior is operated by a commander, driver and gunner, with room for seven soldiers.

MEGA FACT
The M113 was the first 'battle taxi' developed to transport infantry forces on the battlefield.

MARDER APC/AIFV

The first Marders were delivered to the German Army in 1970. Since then, over 3,000 vehicles have rolled off the assembly lines. The all-welded steel hull of this tank provides the driver and troop – a total of eight personnel – with complete protection from small-arms fire and shell splinters. The two-man turret is in the centre of the vehicle, and the troop compartment is in the rear, with two rows of infantry soldiers seated each side. The armament consists of a 20 mm Rheinmetall Mk 20 Rh 202 cannon and a 7.62 mm machine gun. This tank is also has smoke grenade launchers to the left of the cannon.

BTR-60 APC

The Soviet Army unveiled the eight-wheeled BTR-60 just four years after the first in the line of Soviet APCs – the BTR-50P – came into service in 1957. The BTR-60 was the standard APC of the Soviet Naval Infantry (the Soviet Marine Corps). Throughout the 1960s, the BTR-60 was improved until the 8x8 BTR-70 finally replaced it.

RECONNAISSANCE

Reconnaissance vehicles provide the military with important intelligence information. They are sent out ahead of troops and AFVs to survey the local area, secretly observe the enemy and report their findings back to base. Modern reconnaissance vehicles can protect and defend themselves when necessary. They are heavily armoured and carry a variety of weapons systems, including machine guns and mortar weapons.

A CLASS OF THEIR OWN?

The classification of tanks into specific groups, for example, AIFVs, APCs, light tanks and MBTs, can be confusing. What is classed as a reconnaissance vehicle by military officials in one country may be classed as a light tank by officials in another country.

German Panzer Units of WWII

German forces used the first of the Panzer series of tanks, Panzer I, during the invasion of Poland in 1939. During the conquests of 1940–1942, the faster, more powerful Panzer II saw active service. In 1943, the German Army took control of the Italian M15/42 medium tank, designating them PzKpfw III tanks. These formed the bulk of the Panzer Divisionen during the early war years. The Panzer IV – the workhorse Panzer tank – was extremely successful on the battlefield, but a final model, the Panzer V, was developed to counter the threat of the Soviet T–34 model.

MEGA FACT
The Scorpion is also deployed as a light tank in the armies of many countries, including Belgium, Indonesia, Iran, Ireland, Nigeria, Oman, the Phillipines, Spain, Thailand, and the United Arab Emirates.

⊕ **SUPER SCORPION!**
The Scorpion reconnaissance vehicle (shown left), officially the first of the British military's Combat Vehicle Reconnaissance (Tracked) (CVR(T)) series, was developed by Alvis in the UK. The first units appeared in 1972. In 1979, the British RAF Regiment acquired 150 Scorpions in different versions for the protection of air bases in Germany. By 1999, over 3,500 Scorpions had been built for British military use and the export market.

SCORPION

In May 1970, the Scorpion was officially retained for the British Army's reconnaissance units and was designated Combat Vehicle Reconnaissance (Tracked) (CVR(T)). Scorpion vehicles come with a variety of optional equipment, including NBC protection, thermal night-vision equipment, a powered turret, air conditioning and flotation screens. Scorpion vehicles were at the forefront of the 7th Armoured Brigade of the Desert Rats during the 1991 Gulf War. They continue to serve the United Nations peacekeeping forces in Bosnia.

SHADOW RST-V

This 4x4 hybrid electric-drive vehicle with reconnaissance, surveillance, targeting and C3I (command, control, communications and intelligence) capability is coupled with integrated stealth features. The Shadow RST-V can be equipped in a range of mission variants, including air defence, anti-armour, battlefield ambulance, forward observer, light strike, logistics, mortar weapons carrier, personnel carrier and reconnaissance. Bullet-proof windows can also be installed.

BA-64

The BA-64 was the first Soviet armoured car with four-wheel drive. The driver's observation visor was made of removable bullet-proof glass, and the 7.62 mm Degtyarev's machine gun was mounted on a universal machine-gun ring to allow 360 degree rotation. BA-64s and BA-64Bs were used in all major operations and battles of the Eastern Front. A total of 8,174 armoured cars from both types were accepted for the Red Army. The last 62 vehicles were manufactured in 1946.

MEGA FACT
The Scimitar — a variant of the Scorpion CVR(T) — is used by the British Army as an APC to carry specialist troops such as mortar fire control and anti-aircraft personnel.

LUCHS

The German-manufactured Luchs A2 is an 8x8 armoured amphibious reconnaissance vehicle capable of carrying five crew members and a variety of weapons systems. The engine is in a separate compartment at the back, and this is partitioned from the crew's quarters by gas-tight welded bulkheads and fitted with an automatic fire-supression system.

INFANTRY AND COMBAT VEHICLES

The British Royal Navy and the Belgian military were the first to use armoured fighting vehicles (AFVs) with machine guns, in 1914. The interwar period saw the development of six- and eight-wheeled AVFs and half-track vehicles, which had tracks to the rear and wheels at the front. Today, AFVs are used for many military tasks, including air-defence protection, recovery and support vehicles and combat headquarters.

MEGA FACT
The most famous anti-tank gun of World War II was the 88 mm/Flak 41, simply known as 'the 88'. This heavy-duty German weapon was designed and built as an anti-aircraft gun.

MEGA FACT
The first major tank victory since World War II was won by Israel against Egypt during the Suez Crisis in 1956.

M110 — Howitzer

The 203 mm M110-series self-propelled heavy artillery cannon was the heaviest field artillery unit in the US Army and Marine Corps. This mobile howitzer could fire enhanced radiation 'neutron' nuclear warheads, but they did not provide ballistic protection for the 12-man crew. Around 2,000 M110-series howitzers were built in total. The M110A1/A2s, which were active in the Vietnam conflict, superceded the earlier model in the early 1960s. The system was phased out by the US military in the 1990s, but it is still in service with the armies of other nations.

SCOUTING AROUND!

The Bradley Fighting Vehicle System includes the M2 Infantry Fighting Vehicle, the M3 Cavalry Fighting Vehicle and the M6 Bradley Linebacker. Since 1981, around 6,720 vehicles of all types have been deployed by the US and Saudi Arabian armies. The M3 performs scout missions and carries three crew in addition to two scouts. The US Army Bradley upgrade programme includes improvements based on operational experience in the 1991 Gulf War. The first upgrades – the M2A3/M3A3 – entered service in April 2000.

BRADLEY M3

The US military authorised full-scale production of the M2A3/M3A3 Bradley in May 2001 following two years of low-rate production in response to the Bradley upgrade programme. The main armament of the M2A3/M3A3 Bradley is a Boeing 25 mm M242 Bushmaster chain gun. This AFV comes with two M257 smoke grenade dischargers, each loaded with four smoke grenades. The vehicle is equipped with a VTA-903T engine, and the hydromechanical transmission HMPT-500 provides three speed ranges. The engines give a maximum speed of 66 km/h. All Bradleys are amphibious.

MEGA FACT
Welded aluminium and spaced laminate armour protects the hull of the M3 Bradley.

BMP-3

The Soviet BMP-3 is the last in the BMP series of infantry combat vehicles produced in the late 1980s. The tracked, amphibious BMP-3 is designed to engage armoured ground and air targets while stationary, on the move and afloat. The main armament is a 100 mm 2A70 semi-automatic rifled gun/missile launcher. The BMP-3 has a V-shaped UTD-29 diesel engine, which produces up to 500 horsepower. It is still in service with the Russian Army, although it has faced some criticism by military experts.

PIRANHA

The Piranha series of light armoured vehicles was designed by Mowag of Switzerland in the late 1960s. These amphibious vehicles come in a number of different wheel combinations, including 4x4, 6x6, 8x8 and 10x10 configurations. They can protect its occupants against small-arms fire and shell splinters. The Piranha Armoured Combat Vehicle (ACV) is part of the Swedish Navy's coastal artillery brigade.

WARRIOR

Although the APCs designed in the 1960s were capable of performing specialised roles, they did not have the armour or firepower needed to fight on the modern battlefield. In 1986, the Mechanised Combat Vehicle 80 (MCV-80) went into production. Given the name 'Warrior', this APC could protect against indirect artillery fragments, direct machine-gun fire and also offered firepower for general combat support. The Warrior became operational in 1988 and was successfully used by the British Army in the 1991 Gulf War.

AAV
Advanced Amphibious Assault
Vehicle

AFV
Armoured Fighting Vehicle, tanks,
APCs and any vehicle protected
by armour plate.

AIFV
Armoured Infantry Fighting
Vehicle

AMPHIBIOUS
Vehicle capable of travelling on
land and sea.

APC
Armoured Personnel Carrier.
An AFV designed to carry
an infantry squad.

ARV
Armoured Recovery
Vehicle

ATGW
Anti-Tank Guided Weapon

CV
Combat Vehicle

CVRT
Combat Vehicle Reconnaissance
Tracked

FV
Fighting Vehicle

HEAT
High-Explosive Anti-Tank

IFV
Infantry Fighting Vehicle

LAV
Light Assault Vehicle

MBT
Main Battle Tank

MRAV
Multi-Role Armoured Vehicle

NBC
Nuclear, Biological and Chemical

PANZER
The abbreviation of the WW2 *Panzerkampfwagen* - armoured war vehicle. The German word for tank.

RECONNAISSANCE
The act of finding out any information that will help in battle.

SP GUN
Self-propelled gun, artillery mounted on an AFV chassis, which protects the crew and ensures mobility.

SSM
Surface-to-surface missile, any missile launched from the ground against another target also on the ground.

TOW
Tube-Launched, Optically-Tracked, Wire Guided

INDEX

Picture Credits

Front and back cover top (far left), TRH; (centre), MARS; (centre right), TRH; 5, Hulton Archive; 9 (both), TRH; 10 (top), Novosti; 11(bottom), TRH; 15 (top), MARS; 22-24 (all), TRH; 29 (top), TRH; back cover main image, TRH.

All other pictures Alligator Books Limited.